Windows
11

The Good, The Bad
& The Ugly

By

Ojula Technology Innovations

Windows 11: The Good, The Bad & The Ugly

ISBN: 9798479663260

Published in the United States

Limit of Liability/Disclaimer of Warranty

Table of Contents

1. What's New in Windows 11

In this chapter I'll go first over the good features which are the major changes since the Windows 11 insider preview was released. This will be available as a free update to windows 10 users later this year, as long as you meet the system requirements. Now, these requirements could change as quite a few people have been upset about them, since they don't necessarily have all of these requirements but windows 10 runs just fine.

1.1 Windows 11 Requirements

If you meet the below listed minimum requirements, you should be good to go:

- 1 GHZ or faster CPU, dual-core on a compatible 64-bit processor.
- 4GB Ram.
- 64GB storage.
- Motherboard with UEFI and Secure Boot. So, windows 11 cannot be installed on a PC with a legacy bios.
- DirectX 12 compatible graphics.
- TPM 2.0 support (TPM stands for **T**rusted **P**latform **M**odule, a type of processor for preventing malicious attacks on your hardware and boot process).

Initially, Microsoft claimed that Windows 11 wouldn't work on a PC without a TPM 2.0 but it has now confirmed that you can upgrade to Windows 11 without needing TPM 2.0, and that the OS actually requires only the older, much more common **TPM 1.2** module. Microsoft said however that without a TPM 2.0 module you won't be getting the latest security fixes for your brand-new operating system, so you could be opening yourself up to a lot of risk.

Now let's look at what's new in Windows 11 from the custom-built PC that I made.

1.2 The Start Menu, Rounded Corners, Shadows & Power Menu

The first feature that's obviously a good change in Windows 11 is the Start menu. It's now in the middle of the display.

Fig. 1.2.1: The start menu

It can be customized or changed back to the left-hand side if you prefer, but it works great if you have an ultra-wide monitor for example.

They've also added rounded edges to everything. So, if we click on the start menu, for example, you'll see the corners are rounded. There's also some nice sort of shadowing going on behind to give some depth.

Fig. 1.2.2: The Start menu, rounded corners, shadows and Power menu

This looks more like an Android app because we have pinned apps with some new icon designs as well. If you want to see all of your apps, just click on **All apps**. Then you can scroll through all of your apps alphabetically. There are no more live tiles.

You also have the power menu/button in the lower right corner where you can restart or shut down.

1.3 The Desktop

Now on the desktop you can see we have a nice background and some new themes which I'll show you in a moment.

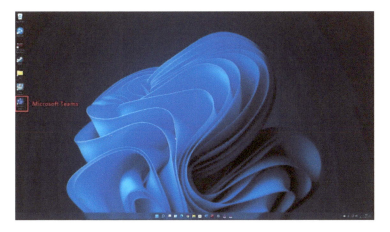

Fig. 1.3.1: The Desktop showing a few icons

If you right click on one of the icons, such as **Microsoft Teams** which is also new and installed on every Windows 11 PC, you'll see they are updated just a little bit. We have **Cut**, **Copy**, **Rename** and **Delete**.

Fig. 1.3.2: The selection window for Microsoft Teams icon, showing the new *Cut*, *Copy*, *Rename* and *Delete* buttons

So, just like you would expect, the desktop hasn't changed much. It's just the visual overhaul.

1.4 The Search

The next icon (on the right of the Start menu shown in Fig. 1.2.1) is the **Search**. If you click on search, you'll see a search bar with *Type here to search* inside, as shown in Fig. 1.4.1.

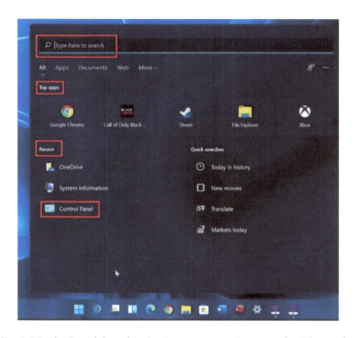

Fig. 1.4.1: The Search box showing top apps, recent apps and quick searches

You will also see your **Top apps**, **Recent** and things like
that. So, just like you would expect, these are your recent
searches or things you've opened before. We also have the
Control Panel. If you click it, you'll see that all of the old
ways to manage your Windows computer are still there.
See Fig. 1.4.2.

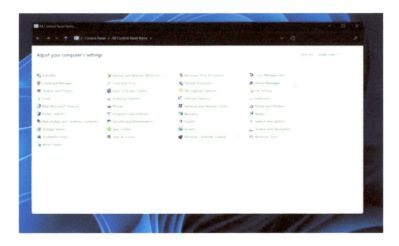

Fig. 1.4.2: The Control Panel window

They're in the background running. If you want to change from small icons to category icons, for example, you can do that. Microsoft haven't removed any of these yet. They're still there if you prefer that. But Microsoft have just visually overhauled everything to make it a little bit easier to use.

1.5 Multiple Desktops

The next feature is the icon shown in Fig. 1.5.1. It's called the **Multiple Desktops** (1). It looks like two gray squares. When you hover your mouse cursor over this icon (or if you use the shortcut **Win + Tab**), it will display all your open programs and all virtual desktops you have created.

Fig. 1.5.1: The Multiple Desktops feature

If you click on the **+** sign inside the **New desktop** preview window (2), you can create multiple desktops with different backgrounds, themes or different applications. You can close any one of these desktops out and switch between them very easily if you prefer to use your computer that way.

1.6 The Widgets

As you can see in Fig. 1.6.1, the next icon is Widgets (1). Microsoft have brought widgets back to windows. Clicking the Widgets icon (1) opens a few widgets, such as Weather, Suggestions, Calendar and Esports (2). We can customize the size of any of these widgets with small, medium or large (3), or even remove them altogether.

Fig. 1.6.1: The widgets in Windows 11

Of course, you can add a widget by clicking the **Add widgets** button in the middle of the widgets window (2). For example, we can add Tips and Sports. We can also resize these widgets to match. As you can see in Fig. 1.6.1, Microsoft have updated widgets so they now look sort of like the live start menu we had before, where we had live news and things like that. But now the widgets are pinned to the left. We can search the web at the top of the widgets window as well (4).

Now, if you have a touch screen, you can slide the widgets (2) in from the left. They've added this sliding feature to widgets just to make it really nice. All the transitions and movements are very smooth, even for an early build.

14

1.7 The Edge Browser & Snap Layouts

This is something they've been talking about quite a lot. It's called the snap layouts. If we click the Microsoft Edge icon (1) at the bottom, and then within the browser, we click the home button, we will arrive at the screen shown Fig. 1.7.1.

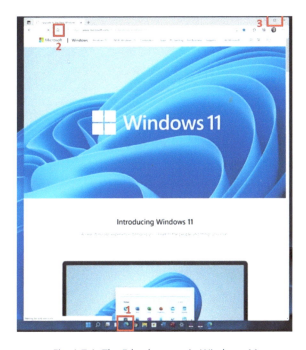

Fig. 1.7.1: The Edge browser in Windows 11

Now, just like in Windows 10, we can click the title bar of the window and drag it any where we like. For example, we can drag it up to make it full screen, or drag and snap it to the left or right.

15

To see available snap layouts from this browser, just hover your mouse cursor over the maximize button (3). A few of these layouts are numbered 1, 2, 3, 4 and 5 in Fig. 1.7.2.

Fig. 1.7.2: A few of the most commonly used Snap layouts in Windows 11

These that are the most commonly used snap layouts in Windows 11. To snap the window to the far left, select the layout **3**. If you have another app like Chrome open, you can snap it to the top right by selecting layout **4**. Open another app again (like the Microsoft store) and select **5** to put it in the bottom right. So, you can just snap things wherever you like. See Fig. 1.7.3.

Fig. 1.7.3: Three apps (Edge, Chrome and Microsoft Store) are snapped to the left, top right and bottom right in Windows 11 respectively

The layouts are also remembered, for example if you connect an external monitor to your computer.

1.8 The File Explorer

The File Explorer is the next thing you can see on the task bar at the bottom of Windows 11. It's been updated just a little bit to match what we have talked about before (rounded corners). We also have new icons (1) shown in Fig. 1.8.1. Everything you would expect is still here though.

Fig. 1.8.1: The File Explorer in Windows 11

1.9 Settings

Instead of the Control Panel, we now have Settings (the gear icon in Fig. 1.7.1). Settings has been dramatically changed and made much easier.

Fig. 1.9.1: Settings in Windows 11

You can see all of my settings in Fig. 1.9.1. You can access anything the old way as well if you're used to that. But on the left, you have everything organized. For example, we have System, Bluetooth & Devices, Network & Internet, Personalization, Apps, Gaming, Accessibility, Privacy & Security and Windows Update.

1.9.1 Windows Update

Windows Update has been updated as well, not only to be faster, but have smaller installs. Microsoft said they'll be updating this on a yearly cycle with new features, not twice a year anymore. Fig. 1.9.2 shows the visual change.

Fig. 1.9.2: Windows Update in Settings of Windows 11

Another good thing about Windows 11 is the consistency they're showing throughout the whole operating system. You can confirm this if you go to System > Display. Also, in Scale and Display Resolution menus, everything's very consistent.

1.9.2 Personalization

Personalization follows themes like we had before.

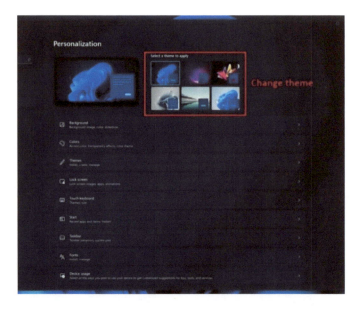

Fig. 1.9.3: Personalization in Settings of Windows 11

We can now very easily change themes. For example, we can switch to a light theme by selecting it from the red box in Fig 1.9.3. As shown in Fig. 1.9.4, you can see everything shifts over to a light theme.

*Fig. 1.9.4: Light theme selected under **Settings > System > Personalization** in Windows 11*

Also, if you want to change the theme, you have more options to add your own wallpaper and sounds for example, because we have new sounds. We also have different colors and everything is customizable, just like you would expect.

We also have different backgrounds, such as "Glow" shown on the top right of Fig. 1.9.5 and a few others.

Fig. 1.9.5: Windows 11 wallpapers showing Windows, Glow, Captured Motion and Sunrise

Another good thing about new Windows 11 is that the wallpapers are very beautiful and are well in contrast with the theme text. You can check out the default wallpapers at this location: C:\Windows\Web\Wallpaper. The default Windows wallpapers have 4K in size, that is, 3840×2400 pixels.

There are 5 categories of wallpapers in the Wallpaper folder:

- Flow
- Glow
- Captured motion
- Sunrise
- Windows

I found more wallpapers in this directory: C:\Windows\Web\touchkeyboard. But these ones have lower size which is 2736×1539 pixels.

Flow is a sort of variation on the light and dark theme we had before. They're all very nice again but I notice some small glitches when I move my mouse over some of these options. However, for an early build, I think they are acceptable.

1.10 Notifications

Now, of course, if we click on our clock and date at the bottom right corner of Windows 11, we can see our notifications like we would expect. There's also a little updated volume icon. When we click on this, we will have the window shown in Fig. 1.10.1.

Fig. 1.10.1: Notifications window in Windows 11 showing updated volume icon

We can see larger buttons for Wi-Fi and Bluetooth, which again are all updated with rounded corners just to match the overall theme. We also have nice animations throughout.

1.11 Windows Security

The security panel shows simply "Security at a glance".

Fig. 1.11.1: Windows 11 Security panel

This is very much like we had in windows 10. For example, we still have the "Virus & threat protection" and "Firewall & network protection" tabs which look basically the same as we had before. So, Windows Security hasn't changed so much, just the rounded corners are updated.

1.12 Microsoft Store

Now they've updated the Microsoft store and the update is fairly significant.

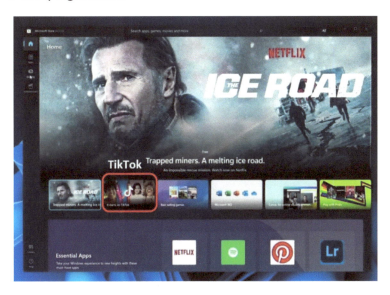

Fig. 1.12.1: Microsoft Store in Windows 11

Not only do we have our gaming with Xbox game pass, we also have auto HDR like we have on the Xbox Series X. They take the different graphics from the games that are not by default set up for HDR and sort of enhance those areas to make them look a little bit nicer.

The biggest change I think is that you can use Android apps within windows 11 through the Amazon AppStore. Now Google Play could bring this later on, that's up to Google. But you can see if we go to TikTOK (see Fig. 1.12.1) that we have Android available, and we can install it on windows 11 and use it here by default.

It doesn't matter what processor you have. It can be an AMD like mine, an Intel or even an ARM processor on a Surface X, for example. Therefore, this should work on all the different platforms natively. You'll be able to use many Android apps as they're released for the device. So hopefully we will see a lot more of those.

Your normal apps are on the Microsoft store as well.

Fig. 1.12.2: Essential apps on Microsoft Store in Windows 11

They are encouraging different companies like Adobe to add their apps here. They are not charging a bunch to add them here. They've also enhanced **touchscreen** support, **voice** and **pen** support with different haptics, for example.

1.13 Device manager and Disk Management

Like I said earlier, there's all of the older features in Windows 11 that you would expect from before. If you go and right click on the start menu, you'll see that we have device manager and disk management for example, just like we had before. The only difference is rounded corners, and the window fades in and out like you would expect. You can do pretty much every other thing you could in Windows 10 here, such as updating a display adapter

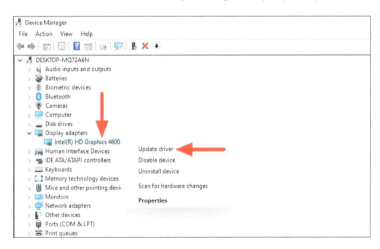

Fig. 1.13.1: Device Manager in Windows 11 showing how to update a display adapter

So, all of the things that you're used to, such as Windows terminal and Computer Management, are still in Windows 11. It's all here. Just like you. It's a really nice update, mostly visual with some nice changes, just for usability.

I think people have been using this at home quite a bit and realizing that it has some downfalls with windows 10, so Microsoft wanted to update it, make it a little bit nicer and easier to use with things like Teams built right in.

So those are all of the major changes within windows. Of course, there are other small changes throughout and they'll continue to update this as it gets closer to its final release.

2. How to Install Windows 11

2.1 How to check if your system can run Windows 11

Quite a few people have asked me to show the way you can check if your PC can run Windows 11. You can download a little application called **WhyNotWin11** (v2.4.1.0). This little application is available for free download at https://www.whynotwin11.com/download/.

When you run on it on your system it will basically tell you whether your system is compatible to run Windows 11. Microsoft had their own health check tool which was available for download at https://www.microsoft.com/en-ie/windows/windows-11. But, at the time of writing, they have pulled it from the internet because it was not working correctly (see it listed as *coming soon* in Fig. 2.1.1).

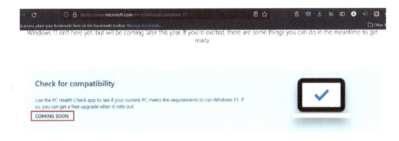

Minimum system requirements

Fig. 2.1.1: Microsoft's page for Windows 11 compatibility check is not available

WhyNotWin11 tool works pretty well, and I'll show you how it works. Basically, once you run it on your system, you will get results similar to the one shown in Fig. 2.1.2 if your system is fully compatible.

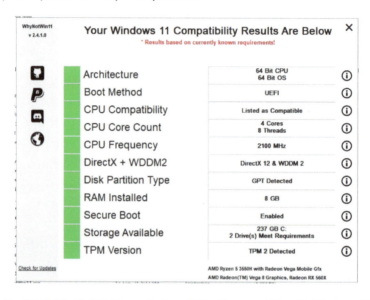

*Fig. 2.1.2: **WhyNotWin11** results for a PC that is compatible with Windows 11*

As you can see in Fig. 2.1.2, WhyNotWin11 gives me OK (with green squares on the left) for TPM version, storage availability, secure boot, Ram, disc partition type, and so on. It gives you all the criteria you need to run a Windows 11 on your system.

As you can see in Fig. 2.1.2, the boot method is UEFI. If you get any sort of yellow or red squares, then your PC may not be compatible for Windows 11. It would look something like Fig. 2.1.3 which is shown with the earlier version 2.3.0.1, though the newer version 2.4.1.0 should give the same results.

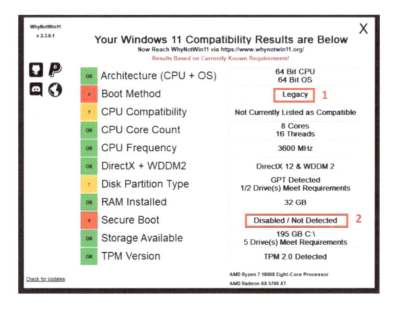

Fig. 2.1.3: WhyNotWin11 results for a PC that is not compatible with Windows 11

You can see here the boot method is legacy (1). So, if you've got legacy mode enabled, your installation won't run.

2.2 Two Methods to Install Windows 11 Step by Step (for Windows and Linux-Based Systems with Backup & Restore Options for Programs and Files)

In this section I'll show you how to install Windows 11 step by step. But before you begin, you should consider backing up your existing Windows 7/8/10 files/data and programs/apps first. To learn how to relocate your existing program files to another drive safely, you need to backup your system in advance. *AOMEI Backupper Standard* is a good and reliable program to do that. Check it out at https://www.ubackup.com/free-backup-software.html.

This article explains details of how to use AOMEI Backupper Standard to do all your backups safely: https://www.ubackup.com/backup-restore/move-program-files-to-another-drive-windows-10.html. You can use this short link instead: https://bit.ly/2Y4aLtf.

Whether you're on a Windows system or on a Linux-based system I'll show you both ways. I'm going to show you two methods:

2.2.1 First Method (Using Windows 11 ISO)

At the time of writing, Microsoft has provided official Windows 11 ISO files for downloading and installing Windows 11. If you have not yet joined the Windows Insider program, then visit the Windows Insider page at https://insider.windows.com/en-us/ and sign in. When you arrive at the registration page, accept the terms of agreement by checking the small box and then click the *Register now* button. Then follow these steps to download and install:

1. Visit this link:

https://www.microsoft.com/en-us/software-download/windowsinsiderpreviewiso

2. Sign in with your Microsoft ID.

3. Under the Selection edition, use the dropdown menu to select the appropriate Windows 11 build you want to download. See Fig. 2.2.1.

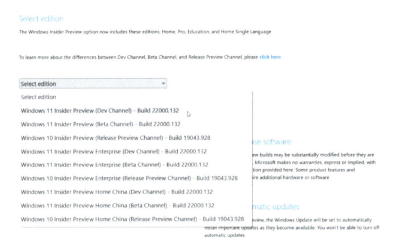

Fig. 2.2.1: Different Windows 11 editions

Fig. 2.2.2 should help you select the right channel for you.

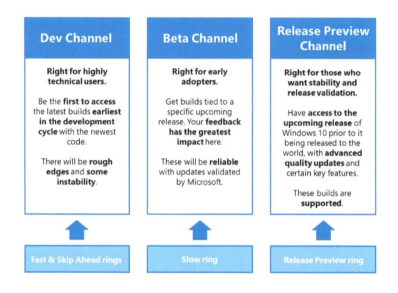

Fig. 2.2.2: About different builds of Windows 11

Click the **Confirm** button to continue. At the time of writing, there are basically two builds of Windows 11:

a. Windows 11 Insider Preview (Dev Channel - Build 22000.132 - less stable)

b. Windows 11 Insider Preview (Beta Channel – Build 22000.132 - more stable)

4. Select your product language such as English, and click the **Confirm** button to continue.

5. You will get on the next screen a link to download Windows 11 ISO. Press the **64-bit Download** button to begin your download. It's important to note that your link is available for only 24-hours from the time you created it. So, you must complete the download process within 24 hours.

Before you install your Windows 11, ensure your system meets all the system requirements discussed I section 2.1 of this book. Visit this link to learn how to bypass some of requirements such as TPM 2.0.

1. Use Rufus to make a bootable USB. Download link is at https://rufus-usb.en.uptodown.com/windows . Alternatively, you can use Ventoy to make your bootable USB. Download link is at https://www.itechtics.com/multiboot-usb-ventoy/.
2. Boot your system using the Windows 11 bootable USB
3. Follow the instructions to install your Windows 11

The installation process is virtually the same as for Windows 10. If you need further help please contact me (email is at the bottom of this book).

Since Windows 11 is still in beta at the time of writing, I strongly advise you should install it on a production system. To check the version after you finished installing Windows 11, just go to **Run –> winver**. You will find out that your Windows is named Windows 11. This implies that this will be the next version of Windows.

Fig. 2.2.3: About Windows 11 version installed

For Linux-based systems, you can't download the windows 11 ISO on a Linux system because of the insider program at the moment. If you've got another computer, you can download the windows 11 ISO as explained above. Open the link below to watch the video made by Britec that shows step by step how to install the windows 11 ISO on a Linux computer.

https://www.youtube.com/watch?v=ZpJdZVOhu1c or use this short link: https://bit.ly/3tOQtiJ

2.2.2 Second Method (Using Windows 10 ISO)

First, you're going to need to download the windows 10 ISO. Here's the direct link to download either the 64-bit or the 32-bit version: https://www.itechtics.com/windows-10-download-iso/.

Windows 10 direct download links

Windows 10 Version 21H1 (Complete changelog and review here)

Download Windows 10 Version 21H1 ISO 64-bit English (5.4 GiB, 146,762 hits)

Download Windows 10 Version 21H1 ISO 32-bit English (3.8 GiB, 24,813 hits)

Fig. 2.2.2: Site to download either the 64-bit or the 32-bit version of Windows 10 ISO

Again, open the link below to watch the video made by Britec that also shows step by step how to install the windows 10 ISO on a Windows computer.

https://www.youtube.com/watch?v=ZpJdZVOhu1c or use this short link: https://bit.ly/3tOQtiJ

3. The Good, The Bad & The Ugly

What Microsoft have made clear is that windows 11 will have fairly restrictive hardware requirements, which will prevent it for being installed on many current PCs. In this chapter, I'll tell you what I think is good, what is bad and what is ugly about windows 11 as we take a quick tour of the new operating system. But before that, I'm going to discuss this issue along with some of the hacks that already emerged.

3.1 A Work Around to Install Windows 11 on Non-Supported Hardware

If you try to install windows 11 on non-supported hardware, you'll soon arrive at this message:

Fig. 3.1.1: Windows 11 Setup error message for non-supported hardware

Since the pre-release versions of the operating system became available, there have been many successful attempts to overcome this problem. For example, when the installer fails at the point shown in Fig. 3.1.1, you simply press **Shift F10** keys to open up a command prompt, and then type **regedit** in the terminal window to enter the registry.

Fig. 3.1.2: Command window is opened when Windows 11 installer fails

Step 1: Navigate to *HKEY_LOCAL_MACHINE > SYSTEM > Setup* as shown in Fig. 3.1.3.

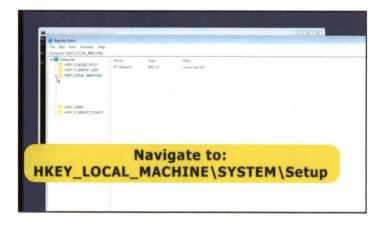

Fig. 3.1.3: How to navigate to HKEY_LOCAL_MACHINE > SYSTEM > Setup

Step 2: Right click on *Setup* to create a new key which we'll call *LabConfig*, as illustrated in Fig. 3.1.4.

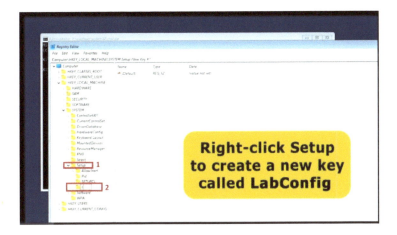

Fig. 3.1.4: How to create a new Setup key called LabConfig

Now, we need to add a new 32-bit DWORD value/name to *LabConfig*. Follow these steps to do this:

Step 3: Right-click *LabConfig* (1) on the left panel, select *New*, and then select *DWORD (32-bit) Value*.

A default name *New Value #1* automatically appears under the name heading on the right.

Step 4: Change this default name to *BypassTPMCheck* (2), as shown in Fig. 3.1.5.

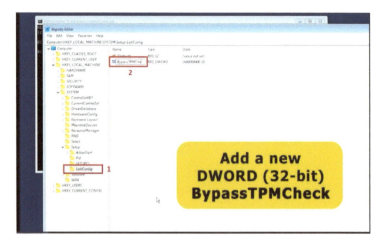

Fig. 3.1.5: How to add a new name (BypassTPMCheck) for our LabConfig key

Step 5: Now right click *BypassTPMCheck* and select *Modify...* to open the *Edit DWORD* window.

Step 6: Enter a value of 1 in the *Value data* filed and click the *OK* button to complete the process. See fig. 3.1.6.

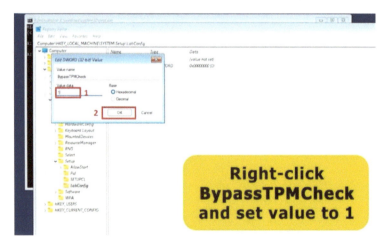

Fig. 3.1.6: How to set a new value (1) for BypassTPMCheck

Repeat **steps 3 to 6** to create another new name called
BypassSecureBootCheck for our LabConfig key and add a
value of 1 again. See Fig. 3.1.7. That is, we right click
BypassSecureBootCheck and select Modify... to open the
Edit DWORD window where we can set a value of 1 for it.
We click the OK button to complete this process as well.

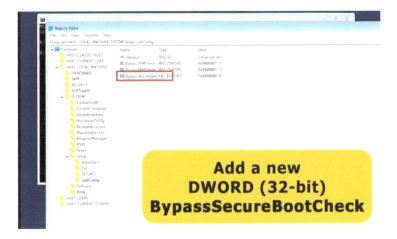

*Fig. 3.1.7: How to add another new name (BypassSecureBootCheck) for our
LabConfig key*

Having completed steps 5 to 6, we can then close the
registry editor window. Type *exit* in the command prompt
window and press enter to close this window too. See Fig.
3.1.8.

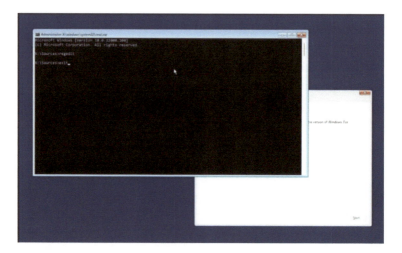

Fig. 3.1.8: How to exit and close the command prompt window

Now if go back to the installer shown in Fig. 3.1.1 above, we'll click the back button (1) on the top left to move back to the previous step of our installation shown in Fig. 3.1.9.

44

Fig. 3.1.9: The previous step of our Windows Setup

We will find out that we can now continue our Windows 11 installation on our non-supported hardware by clicking the *I don't have a product key* button. As illustrated in Fig. 3.1.10, we will click the check box (1) to accept Microsoft's Software License Terms and then click the Next button (2) to continue to the next step.

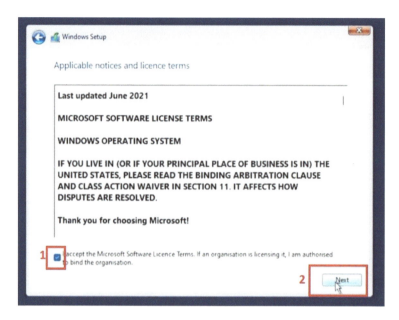

Fig. 3.1.10: The Windows Setup page for accepting Microsoft's Software
License Terms

Now, it's very important to stress that whilst implementing
such registry hacks or any similar work around can make
you feel very smoky. Indeed, what we're actually
experimenting with here is a pre-release version of
windows 11. So far nobody, maybe not even Microsoft,
has got a final version of windows 11 to install, and
therefore nobody can reliably report that they found a
way to install windows 11 on unsupported hardware.

Hacks like those I just shown you should therefore only be
used to assist with temporary Windows 11 installed for
test purposes. To be clear, do not use registry hacks or
similar work arounds to install Windows 11 if you want to

be certain the operating system will continue to run on your system after the final release date.

3.2 How to Dual Boot Your PC with Windows 11 and 10 Step By Step

If you want to play it safe, or maybe you simply don't have a spare PC to try out Windows 11 before you invest your money or resources, you can dual-boot your existing system with Windows 10 and Windows 11 if you have any version of Windows 10 edition on it and switch between them.

In this section I'll show you how to install Windows 11 in its own volume so that each time you boot up your computer, you would then need to choose if you want to use Windows 10 or Windows 11. The most important requirement for a dual-boot setup is that you have sufficient free disk space to install your Windows 11.

A minimum of 25GB of free space is needed, but I strongly recommend you have at least 60GB. Dual-booting your system will take time and effort but once you're done, you'll be able to switch between both. Let's begin.

3.2.1 Preparing Your PC

Before getting started, you must first confirm your PC has the necessary system requirements for Windows 11. How to do this has already been explained in section 2.1. In addition to the fact that you need a TPM 2.0 chip installed in your computer to run this new OS, you may also need to enable the Secure Boot option.

To do this, you need boot up into your BIOS to ensure there is a TPM setting, and that it's set to 2.0. Next, look for a Secure Boot setting and enable it in case it's turned off by default. Since BIOS menus are unique, you may need to check yours on your PC manufacturer's website, or watch a tutorial video made specifically for your own PC model on Youtube.

This article on Microsoft's website may also help you: https://support.microsoft.com/en-us/windows/enable-tpm-2-0-on-your-pc-1fd5a332-360d-4f46-a1e7-ae6b0c90645c, or use this short link https://bit.ly/39IJAX7. So, you don't need to worry if your BIOS looks much different from the one shown in Fig. 3.2.1.

To enter the BIOS setup in most HP computers, you press the power button to turn it on, and then immediately press the Esc (escape key) repeatedly, at least once every second, until the Startup Menu opens. You need to press the F10 function key to open your BIOS Setup.

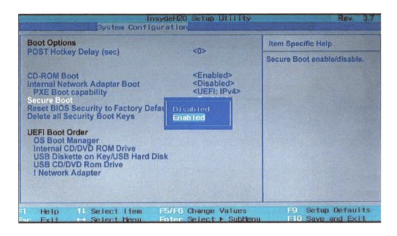

Fig. 3.2.1: The Bios setup showing Secure Boot setting of a HP computer

If the mouse is disabled in your BIOS, use the right arrow key on your keyboard to select the *System Configuration* menu at the top. Then use the down arrow key to select *Boot Options*. Then press the Enter key. Using the down arrow key again on your keyboard, select *Secure Boot*, press Enter, and then use the down arrow key once again to change the setting from *Disabled* to *Enabled*. Press Enter to save the change you just made.

Using the left arrow key, select the *File* menu, and use the down arrow key to select *Save Changes and Exit*. Finally, press the Enter key to select *Yes*. Your system setup utility will close and the system will restart.

3.2.2 How to Download Windows 11 ISO File

But before you begin, you should consider backing up your existing Windows 7/8/10 files/data and programs/apps first. How to do this was already explained at the

49

beginning of section 2.2. Next, you need to download Microsoft's ISO file for Windows 11. How to do this too was already explained in section 2.2.1. If you have not read this section, please go there now to learn how to download your ISO file.

3.2.3 How to Burn Windows 11 ISO File to USB Drive

To install Windows 11, the ISO file must be burned to a DVD. Alternatively, you can copy it to your USB drive and use it later to boot your system. But this process is not simple with Windows 11. Because Windows 11 ISO file is about 5GB, you will not be able to burn it on any standard DVD. Instead, try one 8.5GB or more dual-layer or double-layer (DL) DVD. This should hold the entire file. Alternatively, try a Blu-ray disc, if your computer has a Blu-ray drive.

You might think that using your USB drive is an easier option, but it's not. Since TPM 2.0 and Secure Boot are major requirements for Windows 11, it's not possible to boot a PC with a USB drive that you formatted with NTFS while Secure Boot is turned on. But I'll show you a way around this, though it does involve a bit of work. I highly recommend at least a **12GB USB drive** for this work.

We will prepare your drive for burning by splitting it into two partitions. For the first partition 1, follow these steps:

Step 1: Connect the USB drive to a good USB port on your computer.

Step 2: If you're using a newer version of Windows 10, such as 21H1 Build 19043.1237, you will just right-click your mouse on the Start menu and select **Disk Management**. Otherwise go to **Computer Management** by following this path:

Start button > Windows Administrative Tools > Computer Management > Storage > **Disk Management**.

Step 3: Right-click your USB drive and select **Delete Volume** to erase the drive. See Fig. 3.2.2.

Fig. 3.2.2: How to delete contents of a USB drive in the Disk Management Console

Step 4: Right-click your mouse on the new unallocated space for your USB drive and select **New Simple Volume**. This opens the **New Simple Volume Wizard**. Then click **Next**.

Step 5: Enter 5000 (for 5000 MB) as the size of this volume, which is what this partition requires. Then click the **Next** Button. See Fig. 3.2.3.

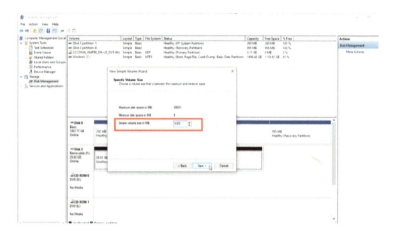

Fig. 3.2.3: How to enter a value for the Simple Volume

Step 6: You should click **Next** at the *Assign Drive Letter or Path* window if you want to accept the default letter, otherwise select a different letter and now click **Next**.

Step 7: At the *Format Partition* window, Change the *File system* to **FAT32** (or **exFAT** if that's what you see there). For *Volume label*, enter any name you want, but I suggest **BOOTPART** since this volume will contain the boot section of the OS, and is also a good label to remember. Click **Next**. See Fig. 3.2.4.

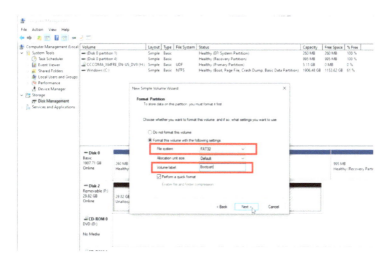

Fig. 3.2.4: How to change the File system and enter Volume label/name

Step 8: In the *Completing the New Simple Volume Wizard* window, you will see a summary of the changes you have made. Finally, click **Finish** to complete the first part of setting up your drive.

We will now work on the second partition. So, for the remaining **unallocated space** in your USB drive, you will now repeat only steps 4 to 8 as follows:

Step 4b: Right-click your mouse on the remaining unallocated space for your USB drive and select **New Simple Volume**. This again opens the **New Simple Volume Wizard**. Then click **Next**.

Step 5b: At the **Specify Volume Size** window, allow the wizard to use **all** the remaining space, and then click the **Next** Button.

Step 6b: Just click **Next** at the *Assign Drive Letter or Path* window if you want to accept the default letter, otherwise select a different letter and now click **Next**.

Step 7b: At the *Format Partition* window, Change the *File system* to **NTFS**. For *Volume label*, enter any name you want, but I suggest **DATAPART** since this volume will contain the data section of the OS, and is also a good label to remember. Click **Next**.

Step 8b: In the *Completing the New Simple Volume Wizard* window, you will see a summary of the changes you have made. Finally, click **Finish** to complete the second part of preparing your drive.

It's now time to reveal all the files in the ISO and also copy them systematically to your drive. Follow the remaining steps below:

Step 9: Open your *File Explorer* to locate the Windows 11 ISO file you downloaded. Right-click on it and select the **Mount** command. This command reveals all the files contained in the ISO as if it were an actual disk. See Fig. 3.2.5.

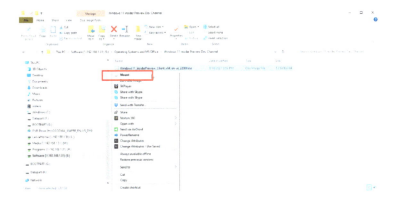

Fig. 3.2.5: How to use the Mount command to open Windows 11 ISO file

Step 10: Once you're inside the ISO file, select and copy all of the files and folders, **except the *sources* folder**, and paste/drop them inside the first partition (FAT32 partition) of the USB drive which we created in steps 1 to 8 above. We will **create our own *sources* folder** in this partition in the next step.

Step 11: Now create a new empty folder on this FAT32 partition and call it *sources*.

Step 12: Open the **original *sources* folder** in the Windows 11 ISO folder in step 10. Scroll to search and copy only the **boot.wim** file inside this folder.

Step 13: Paste/drop the boot.wim file inside your own *sources* folder you created in step 11.

Step 14: Go back to the Window 11 ISO folder to copy **all** the files and folders from there, including the ones you copied before.

Step 15: Paste/drop these files into the second partition (NTFS partition) of your USB drive.

This completes the preparation of your USB drive for burning the ISO file.

3.2.4 How to Create a System Partition for Installing Windows 11 ISO File

In this section you'll learn how to free up some disk space on your PC to create a dedicated partition or volume to install Windows 11. The steps to take are similar to steps 1 to 8 taken above and are as follows:

Step 1: Return to the **Disk Management** console. Under **Computer Management**, right-click on your PC primary drive, which is typically the C drive, and select **Shrink Volume** from the pop-up menu. See Fig. 3.2.6.

Fig. 3.2.6: How to select Shrink Volume for creating a partition on C drive

Step 2: In next window, enter the amount of space you want to make available in the partition. I recommend creating a minimum of 55GB space for your Windows 11. So, enter 55000 and click the **Shrink** button.

Step 3: After shrinking the partition is then shrunk, the amount we entered (55GB in our example) will now show up as our unallocated space. Now right-click on this unallocated space and choose **New Simple Volume** from the pop-up menu. See Fig. 3.2.7.

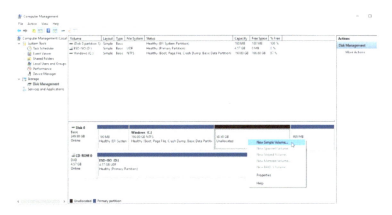

Fig. 3.2.7: How to create a new volume or partition on C drive

Step 4: Just follow the steps the *New Simple Volume* wizard shows you, making sure you accept the default volume in the *Volume Size* window. When the *Assign Drive Letter or Path* window shows up, choose the **Do not assign a drive letter or path** option and then click the **Next** button. See Fig. 3.2.8.

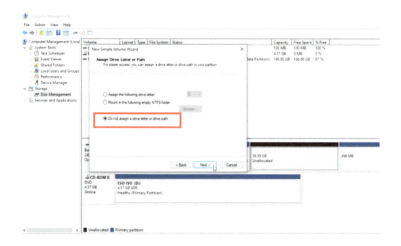

Fig. 3.2.8: The **Assign Drive Letter or Path** window

Step 5: When you arrive the *Format Partition* window, leave the settings for **NTFS** as **Default**. But type Windows 11 Preview, or any name you like, in the **Volume Label** field to identify this volume. Click **Next**, See Fig. 3.2.9. Finally click **Finish** when the next window comes up. You can navigate to *This PC* in your computer to confirm your partition has been created.

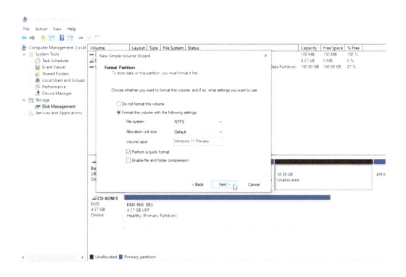

Fig. 3.2.9: The Format Partition window showing how to select the file system and enter the volume label/name

In Step 6 you will reboot your computer. So, before you continue, please copy the remaining steps below to your phone (or take screenshots), another PC or any other location where you can easily open and read them. Also ensure you have a good internet connection and turn it on as it you may want to use it during the installation of Windows 11.

Step 6: While still inserting your USB drive or DVD in your PC, with your Windows 11 ISO burnt on it, reboot your PC, or shut it down first and then start it up again.

Step 7: At the first screen that appears when your computer starts up, press the necessary key, such as **ESC** for many HP computers to access your boot menu (in BIOS setup). Select the drive you want to boot from, such as your USB or DVD drive.

Step 8: The familiar Windows 11 installation screens begin to appear one after the other in this step. It will ask you to do certain things such as:

8a. Choose the right country or region (change or leave default and click **Yes**).

8b. Choose the right keyboard layout or input method (change or leave default and click **Yes**).

8c. If you want to add a second keyboard layout (click **Add layout** or **Skip**).

8d. Name your PC (click **Skip for now** or **Next**).

8e. How you would like to set up the device (select either **Set up for personal use** or **set up for work or school** and click **Next**).

8f. Add your Microsoft account (sign with your email or/and click **Next**).

8g. Create a pin.

8h. Set up a pin.

8i. Restore files from your previous PC or set up this PC as new device.

8j. Choose privacy settings for your device.

8k. Customize your experience on how to get Microsoft recommendations.

8l. Choose to backup or not backup your files with Onedrive.

8m. Other security questions.

8n. And so on...

When you're asked to make any of the above changes or settings, do so or skip those you don't want or unable to do at the moment. You can do most of them later. Just click **Next** or **Skip** in most places.

When a window asking you if you want to install Windows comes up, just click the **Install** button. If you're asked for your product key, enter it if you have it, otherwise just click the **I don't have a product key** link to continue for now (you can enter it later).

After a few minutes, a screen similar to Fig. 3.2.1. will appear. I recommend selecting Windows 11 Pro which is shown selected in Fig. 3.2.1. After making your selection click the **Next** button.

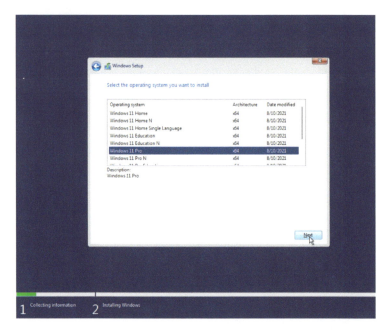

Fig. 3.2.10: Windows 11 setup screen showing a selection of the Windows edition to install

Step 9: Read and accept Microsoft's license agreement terms.

Step 10: At the window where you're asked which type of installation you want to install, choose the second option that says **Custom: Install Windows only (advanced)**. See Fig. 3.2.11.

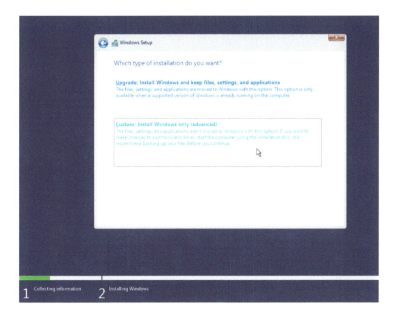

Fig. 3.2.11: Windows 11 setup screen asking you to select the type of installation you want

Step 11: The next window simply asks you in which partition you want to install your OS. Of course, select the *Windows 11 Preview* partition (or the partition you created and named as you like in step 5 above in Disk Management). See Fig. 3.2.12.

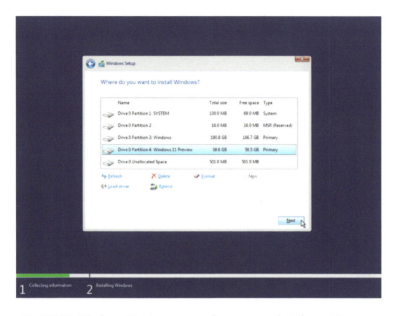

Fig. 3.2.12: Windows 11 setup screen asking you to select the partition you want

Now click the **Next** button. Windows 11 will be installed within 15 to 30 minutes in the new partition if everything is ok.

3.2.5 How to Enroll in Windows Insider Program in Windows 11

After completing the installation, you may be prompted to set up and customize your Windows 11 as you like. When you're done and you have signed into your new operating system as shown in Fig. 3.2.13, it's now time to register with the Windows Insider program. This ensures you keep receiving important updates and insider builds.

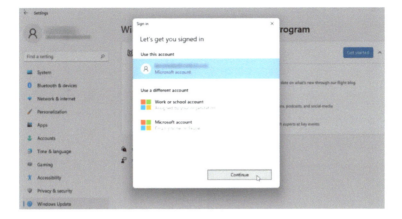

Fig. 3.2.13: Windows 11 Windows Update window asking you to sign in to your Microsoft account

Follow this path to begin:

Settings > Windows Update > Windows Insider Program.

I strongly recommend you allow all necessary diagnostic data to be collected by Microsoft. Click the **Get started** button, and link your Microsoft account for the Windows Insider program. Then click the **Continue** button.

Select your preferred channel, either **Dev Channel** or **Beta Channel**, and then click the **Continue** button. See Fig. 3.2.14. Review the agreement on the next screen and again click **Continue**. Finally click the **Restart now** button to reboot your computer.

Fig. 3.2.14: Windows 11 Insider Channel selection window

3.2.6 How to Set Windows 11/10 Default Operating System

After rebooting your system, you may or may not have seen a boot menu appear upon startup asking you to choose one of Windows 11 or Windows 10 to launch. Didn't see the boot menu? Relax! It doesn't always automatically pop up after one has installed a new operating system like this.

But it's easy to set your own default operating system and change options boot menu when you sign in back into Windows 11. Follow this path:

Settings > System > About

Now click the **Advanced system settings** link. See Fig. 3.2.15.

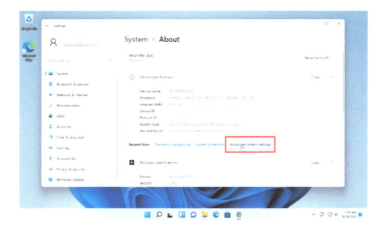

Fig. 3.2.15: How to open the Advanced system settings window in Windows 11

When the **System Properties** window appears, click the **Settings** button next to the **Startup and Recovery** section. See Fig. 3.2.16.

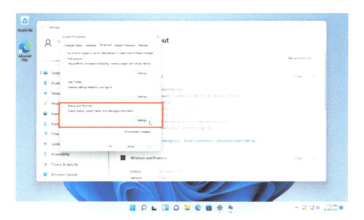

Fig. 3.2.16: System Properties window showing how to open Settings in the Startup and Recover section

When you arrive the Startup and Recovery window, click the drop-down menu under **Default operating system**.

Here, you will see listed both Windows 11 and Windows 10. Select the one you wish make the default every time you start up your system, assuming you don't like manually choosing an operating system.

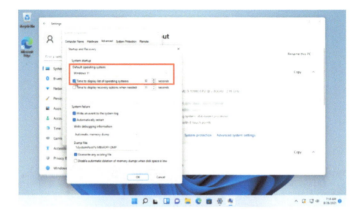

Fig. 3.2.17: Startup and Recover window showing how to set default operating system

Make sure you also check the small box next to *Time to display list of operating systems* and enter the time in seconds that you want the boot menu to show. This will give you sufficient time to choose your preferred operating system. Finally click the **OK** button.

To reboot your PC, click the **Start** button and then select the **Power** menu. Now click the **Restart** button. After rebooting your PC will start up, and the boot menu will appear, asking you to choose between Windows 11 and Windows 10. Just select the OS you want your PC to load. If you don't make a choice, your default operating system will automatically launch after the number of seconds you set has elapsed.

Fig. 3.2.18: Window where to choose the operating system to load

If you want you can change any of the options for the boot menu. To do this, click the **Change defaults or choose other options** link at the bottom. The window shown in Fig. 3.2.19 will come up.

Fig. 3.2.19: Window where to change default boot or choose other options for the operating systems

In this window, you can change the default operating system or change the time before an operating system is launched automatically.

3.3 My Evaluation

As you must have seen, this book it titled "Windows 11: The good, The Bad and The Ugly". So now I will give you my take on what comes under each of these headings. But first, let's see how I evaluated Windows 11.

As I boot into the Windows 11 home edition that I installed on a Pentium gold PC, I discovered that the installation had to be linked to a Microsoft account. I did try very hard indeed to find a way around this, but failed to do so.

After the installation, I notice that Windows 11 has a rather nice default desktop wallpaper. I do have to admit I do quite like the look and feel of windows 11 with its new colors and icons, especially the Start menu.

One of the default applications included in windows 11 is Paint. That's good to see. There've been a lot of discussion recently whether the paint app would disappear in windows but now it's still there. I also see Solitaire. Indeed. I've been playing with Solitaire recently so it's good to have this game included by default. It wasn't included initially in Windows 10 or Windows 8.

We also have the search functionality. It's worth noting that here in Windows 11, we don't have to go to a virtual assistant to open it. It's included by default. I can't tell you how much I (and many other Windows users) love to have easy access to Search. We've also got desktop functionality. So, we can add new desktops and select existing desktops. The search and desktop are both very good features.

Another good feature I see, and which many Windows users have been waiting for, is the widgets panel. This is very exciting. I'm sure you'd like all the sorts of widgets I see coming up in Windows 11.

Two good features that are probably more useful to most people in Windows 11 are the File Explorer and Edge browser, which again, show very nice, quite calm look and feel. I already discussed these in sections 1.7 and 1.8.

If the minimum hardware requirements listed in section 1.1 were the only ones, most current PCs could quite happily run windows 11. But sadly, this is not the case. The reason is that Microsoft has thrown two additional hardware hurdles into the mix. Firstly, windows 11 will not run on just any 1 GHZ dual core 64-bit CPU, but only on one that Microsoft deemed compatible. This is another bad side of Windows 11.

Here are the links to the full lists of compatible AMD and Intel processors have been published on the Microsoft's website:

AMD: https://docs.microsoft.com/en-us/windows-hardware/design/minimum/supported/windows-11-supported-amd-processors, or use this short link: https://bit.ly/2WiXMDb.

Intel: https://docs.microsoft.com/en-us/windows-hardware/design/minimum/supported/windows-11-supported-intel-processors, or use this short link: https://bit.ly/3zMZ5b2.

Another requirement for installing Windows 11 is that it will support only the 8th generation Intel processors or newer. Not only that, Windows 11 will support only second-generation Ryzen (Zen+) AMD chips all later. In practice, this means that any PC with a CPU released before about 2017 for Intel, or 2018 for AMD, will not support windows 11. In turn, this means that a great many PCs sold in 2018 and 2019 will contain a processor that will not be able to run the latest windows operating system. This is at best an absolute disgrace and certainly an aspect of the ugly side of windows 11.

Even if your PC has a compatible processor, Windows 11 also requires it to have a TPM (Trusted Platform Module) and specifically a TPM with 2.0 specification. Microsoft said although you can install Windows 11 on the older, much more common **TPM 1.2** module but without a TPM 2.0 module you won't be getting the latest security fixes, so you could be opening yourself up to a lot of risk. TPMs are crypto processors that help to keep the system safe by placing a hardware barrier around encryption keys and other sensitive data.

The TPM 2.0 standard was set in 2014 and most computers sold in the last few years either have a TPM 2.0 chip on the motherboard, a slot on the motherboard or a TPM module can be inserted, or a firmware TPM included in their CPU. Hence if Microsoft list your PCs processor as compatible with Windows 11, it's likely you will have a TPM available. Note however that you might need to install a bios firmware update to access it, or at the very least, you might have to turn it on in your Bios settings.

To allow people to check if their current PC can run Windows 11, on June 24th 2021, Microsoft launched a health check application. However, the results were so dire for so many users that after a few days it was pulled off. At the time of writing this book (September 2021), it's still listed as coming soon. See Fig. 2.1.1.

Now, the following are my views of the Windows 11 operating system.

3.3.1 The Good Sides of Windows 11

1. Windows 11 is built on the same core architecture as Windows 10, which will maximize software compatibility, an ought to minimize bugs.

2. Also, on the positive side, Windows 11 will only get feature updates once a year! This is a big improvement on windows 10 which likes to stop you working and mess up your PC every 6 months. Who knows in windows 12, Microsoft may revert to providing only necessary security patches. So, we can all get on with just using our computers.

3. Finally, I have to admit that windows 11 looks rather nice, and to my eyes at least, better than windows 10

3.3.2 The Bad Sides of Windows 11

1. On the dark side, like Windows 10 and Windows 8 before it, Windows 11 lacks the precise control of user interface elements that disappeared after Windows 7, and which can still be found in some Linux distributions.

2. The requirement to use a Microsoft account for the Home edition is not good news, as Microsoft continues to take us down the path of an operating system being a service rather than a basic utility.

3. In my view, the Home and Pro or business editions of windows 11 are not widely enough differentiated, with both trying to be all things to all users.

3.3.3 The Ugly Sides of Windows 11

1. Turning to the ugly, the hardware constraints that Microsoft plans to include in windows 11 are shameful. Since Microsoft claim that Windows 11 is faster and more battery efficient than windows 10, it should run at least *as well as* Windows 10 on *existing* hardware.

2. It is a disgrace that Microsoft are trying to force many users to purchase new PCs to run Windows 11.

3. Windows 11's security features really hobble gaming performance. Microsoft is taking yet more backlash over the launch of Windows 11. According to recent reports we received, buyers of new pre-built systems are purportedly losing up to 28 percent of their gaming performance due to frame-rate-crushing security measures. For gamers, this might be a horrible experience. To confirm this, we did several rounds of testing in our lab using some of the best AMD and Intel CPUs for gaming.

We discovered that Windows 11's security mechanisms actually reduce gaming performance. We recorded a range of 10 to 20 percent average impact on one 11th-gen Intel chip. This may not look like much to the untrained eye, but this amounts to roughly an Intel CPU generation's worth of disappearing performance.

4. Windows 10 support ends on October 14th, 2025, and Microsoft's policy clearly states that beyond this date hundreds of millions of computers ought to end up in landfill. Microsoft would I'm sure argue that limiting Windows 11 to PCs with TPM 2.0 and the latest CPUs is good for security and the user experience. But in the home market in particular, it should be up to the user to decide what hardware they consider appropriate and indeed what they can afford.

3.3.4 Apps Experiencing Troubles with Windows 11, and Why Microsoft is Unable to Find a Fix

When Microsoft launched Windows 11 on October 5, 2021, a list of known bugs in their operating system were published. Now customers who are affected by the bugs are unable to install Windows 11 via Windows Update unless they apply a fix or a workaround. Recently Microsoft provided more information about the underlying cause of the problem.

Microsoft says Windows 11 is incompatible with applications that use non-ASCII characters in their registry. The company explains further that such apps might not open and even experience other issues like BOD (blue screen of death). Non-ASCII characters are the symbols, letters and numbers not included in the 128 characters of ASCII. Some good examples are the Japanese and Chinese characters.

To make things even worse, Microsoft says that in some cases, registry keys using non-ASCII characters might also not be repairable. It seems like Windows 11 gets confused when it detects non-ASCII characters in the registry of those apps.

Although Microsoft does not say this on their "Known Issues and Notifications" Dashboard, they have merged it with a previous bug that prevents Cốc Cốc browser users from upgrading to Windows 11. Microsoft has obviously not found a fix for this issue at the time of writing, and that's why they have halted Windows 11 upgrade for users of apps that have non-ASCII characters in their registry.

3.3.5 Eight Windows 11 Troubles Microsoft is currently Investigating

Microsoft is currently investigating the following eight known issues that are caused by software or hardware incompatibilities and which could lead to system crashes or instability. So, here's the full list of eight Windows 11 common issues I discovered so far:

1. Windows 10 taskbar has not been upgraded to the new one designed for Windows 11.

2. Windows 11 Start Menu fails to open.

3. As much as 15% performance drop on AMD CPUs.

4. False "This PC can't run Windows 11" error.

5. Windows 11 File Explorer consumes too much memory.

6. Windows 11 has compatibility issues with Oracle VirtualBox.

7. Dell 'SmartByte' and Intel 'Killer' apps experience slower internet speeds.

8. Windows 11 is incompatible with applications that use non-ASCII characters in their registry.

3.4 Victims of Monopoly

Over 20 years ago, I remember being very excited when I purchased a copy of Windows 98. It was also a positive experience when I moved to Windows XP, and when I purchased Windows 7. However, since that time my enthusiasm for any new version of Windows has waned. Indeed, I think that for many people, Windows is now something they tolerate, rather than crave.

Users of Mac OS or Linux distribution tend to speak very positively about the operating system because they've made a positive choice to use it to deviate from the Microsoft norm. In contrast, many windows users had all made no such choice. They or we are victims of monopoly.

3.5 Conclusion

Now I suspect that due to the hardware requirements, the rollout of Windows 11 will be relatively slow. It'll take quite a long time before lots and lots of people start using it. I also suspect that by 2025, when support for Windows 10 comes to an end, still lots of people will be using Windows 10 or more people will have migrated to Linux.

But what do *you* think about Microsoft's new operating system? Please send me an email to let me know what you think about Windows 11. I'll get back to you quickly. At Ojula Technology Innovations, we hope to put more of books like this out again very soon.

Cheers,

Ojula Technology Innovations

Bolakalearemu2021@gmail.com

www.ingramcontent.com/pod-product-compliance
Lightning Source LLC
LaVergne TN
LVHW072051060326
832903LV00054B/389